Bush Theatre

A Bush Theatre and Antler co-production

Lands

created by Jaz Woodcock-Stewart in collaboration with Leah Brotherhead and Sophie Steer

directed by Jaz Woodcock-Stewart

performed by Leah Brotherhead and Sophie Steer

initial development with Richard Perryman and Nasi Voutsas

6 Nov – 1 Dec 2018
Bush Theatre, London

T0353531

b

Cast

Leah	**Leah Brotherhead**
Sophie	**Sophie Steer**

Creative Team

Director	**Jaz Woodcock-Stewart**
Designer	**Charlotte Espiner**
Lighting Designer	**Rajiv Pattani**
Stage Manager	**Rachel Darwood**
Producer	**Claire Gaydon**

Cast

Leah Brotherhead Leah

Leah last appeared at the Bush Theatre in *The Kitchen Sink*. Her theatre credits include: *As You Like It* (The Lamb Players), *Two Gentlemen Of Verona* (Shakespeare's Globe/Liverpool Everyman), *Wolf Hall & Bring Up The Bodies* (RSC, Aldwych Theatre/The Winter Gardens On Broadway), *Another Place* (Theatre Royal Plymouth), *Pride and Prejudice* (Regent's Park Open Air Theatre), *Doctor Faustus* (West Yorkshire Playhouse/Glasgow Citizen's), *People Like Us* (Pleasance Theatre), *Euphoria* (Ensemble 52), *DNA* (Hull Truck/UK Tour).

TV credits include: *White Gold, Doctors, Vera, Casualty* and *Boy Meets Girl.* Leah is a BBC Carleton Hobbs Award winner and has played numerous roles for the BBC Radio rep company.

Sophie Steer Sophie

Sophie's theatre credits include: *It's True, It's True, It's True* (Underbelly/New Diroama), *Tank* (Breach Theatre, National Tour), *Still Ill* (New Diorama), *Astronauts Of Hartlepool* (Winner of VAULT Festival Origins Award for new work), *Sparks* (Old Red Lion), *Buckets* (Orange Tree Theatre), *Romeo & Juliet* (Watermill Theatre).

TV credits include: *Chickens* (Big Talk Productions).

Short film credits include: *Caliban's Cave, Caliban* and *A Thousand Empty Glasses* (Nominated for Best Short at Raindance/Palm Springs).

Creative Team

Antler Creator

A Bush Associate Artist 2017-18, Antler is an award-winning company, telling stories through theatre and film.

Winner of the IdeasTap Underbelly Award and Pulse Festival Suitcase Prize, nominated for The Stage Best Ensemble Award, and winner of Best Short Fiction at BFI Future Film Festival. Antler have transferred shows to the Bush Theatre, Soho Theatre and toured the UK.

Antler trained on Uri Roodner's Contemporary Theatre Course at East 15 Acting School. Antler was co-founded by Daniela Pasquini, Richard Perryman, Nasi Voutsas and Jaz Woodcock-Stewart.

Previous credits include: *This Way Up* (2012), *Maria 1968* (2012), *Where The White Stops* (2013-2014), *If I Were Me* (2015-2016), *Days Like This* (2016).

Jaz Woodcock-Stewart Director

Jaz is co-artistic director of Antler. She was a finalist for the RTST Sir Peter Hall Director Award 2018. She was also a finalist for JMK Award in 2016 and the Genesis Future Directors Award in 2017. She was recently on attachment at the National Theatre Studio working on a new play, *Wifmon* and has been nominated by National Theatre as part of MITOS21, the European Theatre Network, to workshop a new piece at Performance Laboratory Salzburg 2019.

Theatre credits include: *Lands* (Bush Theatre, UK Tour, Summerhall), *The Bacchae* (East 15), *Civilisation* (Yard Theatre), *Days Like This* (BAC, BeFestival), *You're So Relevant* (Young Vic), *If I Were Me* (Soho Theatre, Underbelly), *Where The White Stops* (Underbelly, Bush Theatre, UK Tour), *Whistleblower* (ObamAmerica,Theatre

503) and *Schoolboy* (Little Pieces of Gold, The Cockpit). Film for Antler credits include: *Emmeline* (short) winner of BFI Future Film Award for Best Fiction.

Staff/Resident/Assistant Director credit includes: *Network*, (National Theatre), *Lazarus* (Kings Cross Theatre), *Adler and Gibb* (Royal Court tour), *Measure for Measure* (Young Vic), *Stink Foot* (Yard Theatre), *Eye of a Needle* (Southwark Playhouse).

Her training is a culmination of time spent on the National Theatre Studio Director's Course, The Jerwood Assistant Director Program at the Young Vic, Uri Roodner's Contemporary Theatre course at East 15 Acting School and Dartington College of Arts.

Charlotte Espiner Designer

Charlotte studied Classics at King's College, Cambridge before training in Set and Costume Design at the Motley Theatre Design School in 2011.

Theatre design includes: *Parents' Evening*, *The Play About My Dad* (Jermyn Street Theatre), *Acis and Galatea* (St John Smith's Square), *Kingdom Come* (RSC), *Summerfolk* (Vanbrugh Theatre, RADA), *Home Chat* (Finborough Theatre), *Adler and Gibb* (Summerhall/ Unicorn/The Lowry/Kirk Douglas Theatre), *It is Easy to be Dead* (Finborough Theatre/Trafalgar Studios), *All or Nothing* (West End/UK National Tour/Vaults), *Mouthful* (Trafalgar Studios), *The Devil to Pay on Brook Street* (Handel House Museum), *Pal Joey* (Karamel Club), *The Dispute* (Summerhall/Odeon Cinemas), *The Winter's Tale* (Bernie Grant's Centre), *The Revenger's Tragedy*, *The Tempest* (Ovalhouse), *This Child* (Bridewell Theatre), *Richard II* (St James' Church), *Hamlet* (The Rose Theatre), *The Provoked Wife* (Greenwich Playhouse), *Entries on Love* (RichMix), *Abstract/Nouns* (Pleasance).

Film design includes: *The Rain Collector* (Wigwam Films), *Lizard Girl* (BBC), *Double Take* (BAFTA/Channel 4), *Paper Mountains* (Ruby Productions), *Copier* (Screen West Midlands Digishorts), *Mirror* (Ruby Productions).

Rajiv Pattani Lighting Designer

Rajiv is one of the technicians at the Bush Theatre, working with Production Manager Michael and the creative teams to realise productions and events in both the theatre and the studio. He is also a lighting designer. Rajiv graduated from LAMDA in 2014 with qualifications in Stage Management and Technical Theatre, specialising in Lighting, Sound and AV.

Recent design work for the Bush includes: the reopening event *Black Lives, Black Words*, *NASSIM* (Traverse 2/ Bush Theatre/International Tour, Edinburgh Fringe First winner 2017), *Ramona Tells Jim* directed by Mel Hillyard, *Hijabi Monologues London.*

Other lighting design credits include: Network Theatre's *STUD* (VAULT Festival 2018), *Screaming Secrets & Glass Roots* (Tristan Bates Theatre), Tom Stoppard's *On the Razzle*, Nina Raine's *Rabbit* (Pleasance Theatre for LAMDA productions), *Blood Wedding* (Bread & Roses Theatre), *Might Never Happen* (Doll's Eye Theatre Company), *Primadonna* (VAULT Festival 2016), as well as various projects at the Arcola, Hampstead and the Unicorn. Rajiv was also Production Electrician on *4 Minutes 12 Seconds* at Trafalgar Studios.

Rachel Darwood Stage Manager

Rachel's theatre includes: *As You Like It* (Shakespeare in the Squares), *Alice in the Cuckoo's Nest, A Christmas Carol, The Book's the Thing* (Librarian Theatre), *Unemployed Actors Union* (Theatre N16), *DARE Festival,*

Phone Home (Shoreditch Town Hall), *The Midnight Gang* (The Chickenshed), *The Divided Laing, A Midsummer Night's Dream, A Steady Rain* (Arcola Theatre).

Since completing her degree at Rose Bruford College of Theatre and Performance in 2014, Rachel has worked on a variety of productions. When not working as a stage manager, Rachel works as a member of the technical crew with ESS Hire, most recently working on the *Jack Petchey Speak Out Finals.* Every year Rachel enjoys going back to the Twinwood Vintage Festival where she works as one of the stage managers.

Thank You
Emily Aboud, Elizabeth Bisola Alabi, Yasmin Hafesji and Salome Wagaine

Bush Theatre

Bush
Theatre
We make theatre
for London. Now.

The Bush is a world-famous home for new plays
and an internationally renowned champion of
playwrights. We discover, nurture and produce
the best new writers from the widest range of
backgrounds from our home in a distinctive corner
of west London.

The Bush has won over 100 awards and developed
an enviable reputation for touring its acclaimed
productions nationally and internationally.

We are excited by exceptional new voices,
stories and perspectives – particularly those with
contemporary bite which reflect the vibrancy of
British culture now.

Located in the newly renovated old library on
Uxbridge Road in the heart of Shepherd's Bush,
the theatre houses two performance spaces, a
rehearsal room and the lively Library Bar.

 Supported by
ARTS COUNCIL
ENGLAND

 h&f
hammersmith & fulham

bushtheatre.co.uk

THANK YOU

The Bush Theatre would like to thank all its supporters whose valuable contributions have helped us to create a platform for our future and to promote the highest quality new writing, develop the next generation of creative talent, lead innovative community engagement work and champion diversity.

LONE STAR
Gianni Alen-Buckley
Michael Alen-Buckley
Rafael & Anne-Helene Biosse Duplan
Garvin & Steffanie Brown
Alice Findlay
Charles Holloway
Miles Morland

HANDFUL OF STARS
Dawn & Gary Baker
Martin Bartle
Charlie Bigham
Judy Bollinger
Clive & Helena Butler
Grace Chan
Clare & Chris Clark
Clyde Cooper
Sue Fletcher
Richard & Jane Gordon
Priscilla John
Simon & Katherine Johnson
Philippa Seal & Philip Jones QC
Joanna Kennedy
V&F Lukey
Robert Ledger & Sally Mousdale
Georgia Oetker
Philip & Biddy Percival
Clare Rich
Joana & Henrik Schliemann
Lesley Hill & Russ Shaw
Team Nelson
van Tulleken Family
and one anonymous donor.

RISING STARS
ACT IV
Nicholas Alt
Mark Bentley
David Brooks
Catharine Browne
Matthew Byam Shaw
Tim & Andrea Clark
Sarah Clarke
Claude & Susie Cochin de Billy
Lois Cox
Susie Cuff
Matthew Cushen
Philippa Dolphin
John Fraser
Jack Gordon & Kate Lacy
Hugh & Sarah Grootenhuis
Jessica Ground
Thea Guest
Patrick Harrison
Ann & Ravi Joseph

RISING STARS (continued)
Davina & Malcolm Judelson
Miggy Littlejohns
Isabella Macpherson
Liz & Luke Mayhew
Michael McCoy
Judith Mellor
Caro Millington
Mark & Anne Paterson
Pippa Prain
Barbara Prideaux
Emily Reeve
Renske & Marion
Sarah Richards
Julian Riddick
Susie Saville Sneath
Saleem & Alexandra Siddiqi
Brian Smith
Peter Tausig
Guy Vincent & Sarah Mitchell
Trish Wadley
Amanda Waggott
Alison Winter
and three anonymous donors.

SPONSORS & SUPPORTERS
AKA
Alen-Buckley LLP
Gianni & Michael Alen-Buckley
Jeremy Attard Manche
Bill & Judy Bollinger
Edward Bonham Carter
Martin Bowley
Duke & Duchess of Buccleuch
The Hon Mrs Louise Burness
Sir Charles & Lady Isabella Burrell
Philip & Tita Byrne
CHK Charities Limited
Peppe & Quentin Ciardi
Joanna & Hadyn Cunningham
Leo & Grega Daly
Patrick & Mairead Flaherty
Sue Fletcher
The Hon Sir Rocco Forte
The Hon Portia Forte
Mark Franklin
The Gatsby Charitable Foundation
The Right Hon Piers Gibson
Farid & Emille Gragour
Victoria Gray
John Gordon
Vivienne Guinness
Melanie Hall
The Headley Trust
Brian Heyworth
Lesley Hill & Russ Shaw

SPONSORS & SUPPORTERS (continued)
Michael Holland & Denise O'Donoghue
Graham & Amanda Hutton
James Gorst Architects Ltd.
Simon & Katherine Johnson
Tarek & Diala Khlat
Bernard Lambilliotte
Marion Lloyd
The Lord Forte Foundation
Peter & Bettina Mallinson
Mahoro Charitable Trust
James Christopher Miller
Mitsui Fodosan (U.K.) Ltd
Alfred Munkenbeck III
Nick Hern Books
Georgia Oetker
RAB Capital
Kevin Pakenham
Sir Howard Panter
Joanna Prior
Josie Rourke
Lady Susie Sainsbury
Barry Serjent
Tim & Catherine Score
Search Foundation
Richard Sharp
Susie Simkins
Edward Snape & Marilyn Eardley
Michael & Sarah Spencer
Stanhope PLC
Ross Turner
The Syder Foundation
van Tulleken Family
Johnny & Dione Verulam
Robert & Felicity Waley-Cohen
Elizabeth Wigoder
Phillip Wooller
Danny Wyler
and three anonymous donors.

TRUSTS AND FOUNDATIONS
The Andrew Lloyd Webber Foundation
The Boris Karloff Foundation
The Boshier-Hinton Foundation
The Bruce Wake Charitable Trust
The Chapman Charitable Trust
The City Bridge Trust
Cockayne—Grants for the Arts
The John S Cohen Foundation
The Daisy Trust
The Equity Charitable Trust
Eranda Rothschild Foundation
Esmée Fairbairn Foundation
Fidelio Charitable Trust

TRUSTS AND FOUNDATIONS (continued)
Foyle Foundation
Garfield Weston Foundation
Garrick Charitable Trust
The Harold Hyam Wingate Foundation
Hammersmith United Charities
Heritage of London Trust
The Idlewild Trust
John Lyon's Charity
The J Paul Getty Jnr Charitable Trust
The John Thaw Foundation
The Kirsten Scott Memorial Trust
The Leche Trust
The Leverhulme Trust
The London Community Foundation
Margaret Guido's Charitable Trust
The Martin Bowley Charitable Trust
The Monument Trust
The Noel Coward Foundation
Paul Hamlyn Foundation
Peter Wolff Foundation
Pilgrim Trust
The Royal Victoria Hall Foundation
The Theatres Trust
Viridor Credits
The Williams Charitable Trust
Western Riverside Environmental Fund
Worshipful Company of Meccers
The Wolfson Foundation
and one anonymous donor.

CORPORATE SPONSORS AND MEMBERS
The Agency (London) Ltd
Dorsett Shepherds Bush
Drama Centre London
The Groucho Club
THE HOXTON
Westfield London

PUBLIC FUNDING

If you are interested in finding out how to be involved, please visit **bushtheatre.co.uk/support-us** or email **development@bushtheatre.co.uk** or call **020 8743 3584**.

LANDS

LANDS

by Jaz Woodcock-Stewart with the company

OBERON BOOKS
LONDON

First published in 2018 by Oberon Books Ltd
521 Caledonian Road, London N7 9RH
Tel: +44 (0) 20 7607 3637 / Fax: +44 (0) 20 7607 3629
e-mail: info@oberonbooks.com
www.oberonbooks.com

A catalogue record for this book is available from the British Library.

PB ISBN: 9781786825698
E ISBN: 9781786825704

Cover design: Studio Doug

eBook conversion by Lapiz Digital Services, India.

*For my Dad, who taught me about
words and stories and ideas*

Acknowledgements

I am in debt to a few good women:

To my collaborators and actor-dramaturgs, Leah and Sophie.

To Claire Gaydon, without whom none of this would have happened.

To Charlotte Espiner.

Also

To my Antler co-founders, Richard and Nasi, for beginning this with me.

To my parents, for whom the phrase 'unwavering support' must have been invented.

To Madani, Omar and the Bush for giving Antler a home, from our first piece at RADAR in 2013 to bringing us on as Associate Artists, and continuing to support the conversation about what new writing can be.

Further thanks to

Bethany Haynes and BAC, David Byrne, Sophie Wallis, Helen Matravers, Ellie Simpson and New Diorama. Jessi Stewart, Summerhall, Sue Emmas and the Young Vic, Hannah Smith, Joel Horwood, Morgann Runnacre-Temple, Bryony Shanahan, Yasmin Shamolzadeh, Heather Stewart and Mark Woodcock, Daniel Foxmith, Alex Brenner, Meurig Marshall, Stewart Pringle, Deirdre O'Halloran.

Notes on *Lands*

The script is not sacred, it's a blueprint for performance. The words should feel comfortable in the mouths of the performers. If they don't, change them.

Something that is important, however, is rhythm and space which I have tried to articulate in this text. Dots, for instance, give some indication of the length of a pause.

Lands is not a play in the traditional sense. Creating it involved different processes: some of it written, some of it improvised by the actors, written down and edited, and some of it improvised each performance, the nuances of which are virtually impossible to document.

Some sections are 'locked', in which the words spoken are the ones written here, accurate not only to the word but to the beat. And some are 'unlocked', where we agreed on structures and rules within which the performers could move.

A few examples that are 'unlocked':

- **Page 35-36** – Repeat '*AND GO*' as many times as you feel. Play the game of this. Play with variations of '*AND GO*'. Keep the same rhythm, listen and respond to what the other person offers. Embrace repetition.

- **Page 38** – The ending of this section is not fixed. Leah returns to the '*5, 4, 3, 2, 1*' countdown, repeating and getting carried away with it until Sophie stops her. Play and repeat as you feel.

- **Page 29** – Repeat the '*What do you mean*' lines if needs be. Take as long as it takes to control laughter. Once laughter is contained, it is Leah's job to win Sophie back round. They can both say what they need to say in order to negotiate this corner. This will vary every time.

- **Page 42** – '*I'm fine/You're not fine*' and **Page 56** – '*You don't understand/You don't understand*'– Performers are only allowed to say these phrases (or variations of these phrases) to each other. Play this game, listen and respond as you feel. Push this for longer than is comfortable.

- **Page 63** – Play with a real stopwatch/phone timer and adjust text and times as necessary.

With the '*I don't care*' speech on **page 56-62**, there should be a peppering of specific references to recent events. I have marked these in the playtext with an asterisk. You may want to add lines relevant to the place or circumstance in which you are performing. Adapt as you will.

If you do explore changes to the text, press always for economy of expression. Keep references open. Don't refer to the puzzle as the puzzle and the trampoline as the trampoline. Try to keep the piece in between a somewhere and a nowhere.

Puzzle

The details of each piece of the puzzle should be improvised by the performer taking Leah's part. It is a task-based exercise. Describe the puzzle piece as you see it to the audience, as fully as possible. Hypothesise about the possibilities of what the bigger picture could be. The performer should not know what the picture on the box is.

Some puzzles are more useful than others. Find a puzzle with a lot going on. A busy, populated scene. For reference, we used Mike Jupp's I Love the Country. Equally, some puzzle pieces are more useful than others. It may be useful to rig the system.

In the playtext, sections in **bold** indicate puzzle improvisation. These examples are included to give the reader/performer a sense of it.

Further Puzzle Instructions

Say the piece number. Say what you see. What are the main features of the piece? Describe in detail. Is it clear straight away what the piece is? Try and challenge your own assumptions about what a piece might be. If it's not clear, list all options. Are there any distinguishable objects? People? Characters? Feature colours? Sizes and proportions? If more than one element, how do they relate each other? Does it relate to previous pieces you've found? Push yourself to find unconventional or darker interpretations of the piece. Ask yourself questions out loud: What are the questions within the questions? What are the implications for the bigger picture? What might the bigger picture be? What are some areas for further investigation? There is no right or wrong. Follow instincts, follow stream of consciousness. Try not to be funny, interesting or original.

Names

In our production, Sophie and Leah used their own names. For ease, we have continued using their names in the playtext. Please substitute your own names when performing the text. There is no character of Sophie and there is no character of Leah, there is only the person playing the situation and speaking the words.

They are women in our production but gender is not implicit to the parts. You can be any gender to perform this text. Please adjust names and pronouns to suit your cast.

Similarly we have used the name of our stage manager in the playtext. Please replace with the name of the person operating your sound and lights.

Music

The music choices are significant to us and our production but please feel no reverence towards them.

Audience

You are in the same room as the audience. It's important that you see them. Embrace this.

0. PRESET

'You and Me Part II' by Fleetwood Mac plays.

LEAH works on the puzzle.

SOPHIE jumps on the mini trampoline.

LEAH works at a puzzle station. She has her working puzzle in front or her. In the stage directions, we will call this the 'Working Puzzle'. Not too far away, she has a previously completed puzzle. We will call this the 'Masterpiece Puzzle'. She has completed many puzzles in the past, but in our production these are the only two onstage. Her puzzle station is lit by a desk lamp.

SOPHIE peels and eats a tangerine whilst jumping.

1.

SOPHIE continues jumping.

LEAH holds each piece up to the light of the lamp. She talks into a microphone to the audience, detailing the composition of each piece. The pieces are selected at random, and the text is improvised. See notes for more details.

LEAH   **Piece 112. Mainly features a red telephone box. A man is inside it. A queue of two people outside. That's a long queue for a phone box in this current age of mobiles. I've not seen a queue like that since the mid-90s – is this a clue as to when the picture is set? Could be, could be. It could be a freak accident that these three people happen to have left their mobiles at home today – who are they ringing? Just a casual call? Are they ringing someone at home to bring their mobile to them? Are they making prank calls? It *would*** be an ideal phone to use. More pieces needed still to determine the decade, that could certainly help clear this up.

Piece 113. Glamorous woman! Beautiful hair, black. Sunglasses on. This would indicate it's a sunny day. I have seen some very blue sky pieces. This helps strengthen that theory. Oh wait and she's in a convertible car, roof down. Hello summer. Or perhaps a bright spring day, slight chill still in the air. She could be hungover and has got the roof down to get the wind in the face, get fresh! That truck is incredibly close to her, right up her back – heavy traffic – traffic at a stand still? Busy city centre? Or just dangerous driving? Further car pieces needed to determine traffic status... Interesting though...

SOPHIE finishes the tangerine and throws the peel on the floor.

Piece 114. Mainly features...a bomb. Jesus! I wonder if anyone knows. I don't think they have any idea. It seems to be in a field. This must be a background piece, it's in a background field. Clever, very clever. No one is aware of this perhaps impending doom. Christ. It could be an unexploded WW2 bomb. Hopefully some trained persons shall be out there dealing with it soon.

SOPHIE   D'you know what it is yet?

LEAH   No, not yet.

But I'm getting closer.

2.

SOPHIE is drinking from a bottle of water whilst jumping.

SOPHIE   – and of course the owner says, 'It's a 10 out of 10', and of course she says, 'I think it's amazing, I love everything on the menu.' I mean she wouldn't be on the programme in the first place if she was self-aware so this all makes perfect sense. This is the classic answer.

So the owner leaves, the waitress comes over, and he asks the waitress what the soup of the day is. And she says, (it's awful, it's something awful, it's like – it's very American – jalapeños, that's it – jalapeño corn chowder) 'Jalapeño Corn Chowder', and he goes, 'Okay great, and what was the soup of the day yesterday?', 'Jalapeño Corn Chowder', 'So it's soup every two days', he says. And she goes, 'And last week...', 'So it's soup of the week, then.' He says, like very dry, very – and then – basically – next thing, he's called the owner back over and he says to her, 'Can I just let you into a little secret? Not in front of your customers, can I whisper?' And he makes her bend down and he leans in and he does this awful sort of patronising whisper in her ear: 'Soup of the day is not soup of the day. You're serving the same soup that was on two weeks ago.' And she's like – she really doesn't understand what's happening, but she's still bending over, she's still in this sort of semi-bend and she whispers back, 'What do you mean?' And he says, 'Soup of the day means a Daily Changing Soup.'

SOPHIE throws the bottle of water to LEAH – LEAH catches it and places it down.

LEAH notices the orange peel on the floor, stares at it.

And this has just blown her mind. She doesn't
understand, she's never understood, she's
mortally embarrassed, she goes, 'Oh. I thought it
just meant what soup we were serving that day…'
'Soup of the day.' He says it again, 'A new soup
every day.'

LEAH   Sophie

SOPHIE   Of course, when the soup does eventually turn
up, he looks at it, pokes at it with his spoon then
says, 'That's just slop. Horrible nasty gloop.'

LEAH   Sophie

SOPHIE   Yeah?

What?

What?

LEAH   Sophie

SOPHIE   What, I'm saying what.

LEAH   What am I looking at?

SOPHIE   Oh

Shit, sorry.

.

.

.

.

LEAH is still looking at her.

What?

LEAH   And then?

SOPHIE   And then?

LEAH   Sorry and then?

SOPHIE   Sorry and then…

LEAH   And then –

SOPHIE   What?

LEAH   .

SOPHIE   Put it in the bin.

LEAH   Yes!!

SOPHIE   Oh!

         Yes.

         I'm sorry I'll put it in the bin.

LEAH   Fine.

         .

         .

         .

         .

         .

         .

         .

         .

         .

         .

         .

         When?

SOPHIE   What?

LEAH   When are you going to put it in the bin?

SOPHIE   In a bit

LEAH   Can't you do it now?

SOPHIE   Can't right now

          .

          .

          (Opening a can of worms.) I don't mind it.

LEAH   *(A look that says: 'Do you really want to go there?')*

SOPHIE   I'm sorry I'll put it in the bin in a bit.

          .

          .

          .

          .

          .

          .

          .

          .

          .

          .

LEAH   Oh for god's sake.

          LEAH gets up and puts it in the bin.

          Returns to the puzzle.

          Unbelievable.

.

.

.

.

.

SOPHIE   I would have done it.

If you'd let me.

3.

LEAH back at the puzzle. Finding a piece:

LEAH   Here she is. Here she is. Here she is. Yes. Yes. Yes. Yes. It's a connection. Completion of **video rental store sign**.

LEAH looks at Rachel who is operating LX and sound in the tech box.

Rachel.

'Ain't that Terrible' by Roy Redmond plays. LEAH begins her celebration dance. SOPHIE joins in. They perform the same moves. SOPHIE performs the routine on the trampoline.

LEAH returns to doing the puzzle.

Piece 129. Mainly features an extreme close up of…**teeth**.

4.

LEAH   **Looks like four men in a car, threatening looking men. I would not – it's a red car. More transport here. More transport. Where are they going?**

> **Where have they been? Why do they look threatening? It's a look, it's a feeling. Oh! What's he holding?**

Her desk lamp goes off. She tries to turn it back on. It is broken.

> Shit.

> Fuck. Shit.

> .

> .

> .

> .

> .

> .

> .

> .

> .

> .

> Sophie?

SOPHIE   Yeah.

LEAH   Will you come and have a look at this and tell me what you think this is?

> .

> .

> .

> .

SOPHIE   What?

LEAH   Will you come and have a look?

SOPHIE   Come and have a look?

LEAH   Yeah.

SOPHIE   And tell you what I think it is?

LEAH   Yeah.

.

.

.

.

SOPHIE   You don't want me to

LEAH   I do.

SOPHIE   Do you?

LEAH   Yes.

SOPHIE   Do you though?

LEAH   Yes.

.

.

.

.

.

.

.

SOPHIE   I've seen it.

LEAH   You've seen it?

SOPHIE   Yes.

LEAH   When?

SOPHIE   What?

LEAH   When have you seen it? You've never seen
         anything. You've never seen any of them. Oh my
         god.

         .

         .

         .

         When have you seen it?

SOPHIE   Earlier.

LEAH   What d'you mean earlier?

SOPHIE   I came up behind you and looked over your
         shoulder.

         .

         .

         .

         It is looking great.

LEAH   You came up behind me and looked over my
         shoulder.

SOPHIE   Yes.

LEAH   Why didn't you say?

         .

         .

Why didn't you say what you thought – what you
thought it was? Why didn't you say what you
thought of this masterpiece?

She walks over to the Masterpiece Puzzle.

(To the puzzle.) You were my hell and my salvation.

.

.

Sophie?

SOPHIE   I did.

I did say something. I said it quietly.

I whispered it.

LEAH   You whispered it??

SOPHIE   Yes

LEAH   Why did you whisper?

SOPHIE   Didn't want to –

LEAH   What did you say?

SOPHIE   Oh I can't really remember, *(whispering)* 'Oh
Leah, that looks really good.'

LEAH   You came up behind me, you looked over my
shoulder and you whispered in my ear, 'Oh Leah,
that looks really good'???

SOPHIE   Yeah

LEAH   That's a bit creepy.

SOPHIE   Is it?

LEAH   Yeah.

Bit creepy. Bit sneaky. You having a sneaky peaky?

SOPHIE   Maybe

              .

              .

LEAH   Well what did you think?

SOPHIE   Of what?

LEAH   The picture.

SOPHIE   Yeah loved it.

LEAH   All of it?

SOPHIE   Yeah.

LEAH   What did you love about it?

SOPHIE   I really loved – I really loved – all the pictures
           inside the picture, y'know?

LEAH   Yeah, yeah, yeah, yeah

           What did you think of the top right corner?

SOPHIE   That was my favourite bit.

           It was the warmest, kind of…sweetest bit I guess.
           Made me feel, made me feel sort of – nostalgic.

LEAH   Top right?

SOPHIE   Yeah.

LEAH   That's a man being stabbed.

              .

              .

              .

              .

              .

SOPHIE   Hmm?

LEAH   Top right? That's a man being stabbed in the
          neck. There's blood gushing out of his neck and
          all down his shirt.

          .

          .

          .

          You think it's the warmest sweetest bit? That was
          your favourite bit?

          .

          .

          .

          .

          .

          .

SOPHIE   Yeah.

LEAH   It made you feel nostalgic??

SOPHIE   .

          .

          .

          .

          Yeah.

          .

          .

.

.

.

In a way.

.

.

.

LEAH   I – I didn't experience it like that.

SOPHIE   Where there's dark, there's light…

LEAH   Are you…

Ok.

Look, can you just come and have a look at my new one?

SOPHIE   I can see it from here. Honestly I can see it from here.

LEAH goes over to the trampoline.

LEAH   You can't see anything from here.

SOPHIE   No from here. *(Bouncing higher.)* From here. From here. You can see loads from here. I can see – oo is that a milkmaid?

LEAH   *(Going back to the to Working Puzzle.)* The milkmaid! You can see a milkmaid! I've been looking for her I've been looking for her. Where is she?

(She takes the Working Puzzle over to SOPHIE.) Where is she? Where is she Sophie? If you could *(handing the board to SOPHIE and going back to the station)* because actually! I thought I saw one of the –

SOPHIE is left bouncing on the trampoline with LEAH's Working Puzzle. The puzzle pieces go everywhere. SOPHIE is left with an empty board.

5.

The majority of pieces are on the floor. A couple of pieces may have landed on the trampoline.

LEAH stares at SOPHIE. SOPHIE feels LEAH's stare.

SOPHIE   *(Handing the empty board to LEAH.) I've got it.*

SOPHIE attempts to pick up the pieces on the trampoline by bouncing hard until they bounce high enough for her to catch them. She does this successfully once, twice and then –

Sometimes it's really good to just get them all out there. Get a different perspective.

LEAH   That took me three hours.

.

.

.

LEAH starts to pick the pieces up off the floor. SOPHIE jumps on the trampoline.

Are you going to give me a hand?

.

.

.

Sophie, come and pick them up. You threw them everywhere.

.

.

.

Ok.

LEAH carries on picking up pieces.

.

.

.

.

.

.

Are you seriously not going to pick the last few pieces up? You're not going to pick anything up?

.

.

.

SOPHIE is unresponsive.

Sophie, pick the last two pieces up.

.

.

.

.

Sophie

Sophie

Sophie

SOPHIE   Yep.

LEAH   Pick up the last two pieces.

SOPHIE unresponsive.

LEAH goes back to fixing her puzzle.

6.

SOPHIE   I can't.

.

.

.

.

.

.

.

I can't

Leah

Leah

LEAH   What?

SOPHIE   I can't

LEAH   Can't what?

.

.

.

What?

SOPHIE   I can't…

Get off.

LEAH   Ok.

        .

        .

        .

SOPHIE I can't – I can't get off

        I'm stuck

LEAH   You're stuck

SOPHIE I'm stuck on the thing I'm stuck on the thing I'm
        stuck on the thing

        .

        .

        .

LEAH   *(Smiles.)*

SOPHIE Don't

        .

        .

        Don't

LEAH   Are you joking? Just get off it.

SOPHIE Please

        Don't

LEAH   I'm not doing anything

SOPHIE .

LEAH   Just get off it

Sophie

Sophie

Just get off it

Are you actually being serious?

SOPHIE YES OF COURSE I'M BEING SERIOUS I'M
STUCK ON THE THING, I'M STUCK ON THE
THING

LEAH JUST GET OFF IT. JUST GET OFF IT.

SOPHIE I can't get off I can't get off I can't get off I can't get off
I can't get off I can't get off I can't get off I can't get off
I can't get off I can't get off I can't get off I can't get off
I can't get off I can't get off I can't get off I can't get off
I can't get off I can't get off I can't get off I can't get off

LEAH finds this funny.

STOP FUCKING LAUGHING AT ME

*This sets LEAH off. She finds it extremely hard to contain
her laughter.*

SOPHIE turns away.

LEAH, attempting and failing to contain laughter –

LEAH What d'you mean?

.

.

.

What d'you mean you can't get off?

.

.

．

(Regaining composure.) No, I'm sorry.

．

．

．

No I'm thinking now. What d'you mean you can't get off? *(Laughing again.)*

SOPHIE I'm never talking to you again.

LEAH No, Sophie. I'm here. I am here. I'm here. I'm here now.

7A.

LEAH When was the last time you got off it?

SOPHIE Can't remember

A long time ago

LEAH You have been off it, you've been off it

SOPHIE No

No

．

．

．

．

．

But that's –

It's good, actually. It doesn't – Which bit were you working on? It was the taxi rank wasn't it? Oh yeah! You'd found the –

LEAH   I can't remember the last time you were off it.

SOPHIE No but

LEAH   I haven't seen you off it.

        Sophie, I haven't seen you off it.

SOPHIE Let's not

LEAH   Why can't you get off it?

SOPHIE .

        .

        .

        .

        Erm

LEAH   Do you want to get off it?

        .

        .

        .

        .

        .

        Do you want to get off it?

SOPHIE Yes.

LEAH   Do you?

SOPHIE Yes.

LEAH   Ok

Let's get you off then...

(Walking towards SOPHIE to pull her off.) Let's get you off it.

SOPHIE   WOAH WOAH woah woah woah.

Not like that. Not like that.

LEAH   Ok, let's try something else. Ok. Ok, let's think, what could we do?

We're going to do a countdown.

LEAH takes the mic off the mic stand.

We're going to do a countdown and then you're gonna *(she gestures jumping off without saying it).*

Let's just rip off the plaster.

SOPHIE   Ok. Great.

Can we rip it off tomorrow?

LEAH   I think we should do it now.

You ready?

SOPHIE   .

.

.

.

.

Yes.

.

.

.

LEAH	5
	4
	3 –
SOPHIE	From 10. From 10
LEAH	From 10.
	10
	9
	8 –
SOPHIE	From 20.
LEAH	No we're not doing 20, that's too long.
	Ok 10?
SOPHIE	Ok 10.
LEAH	Ready?
SOPHIE	Yep.
LEAH	10
	9 –
SOPHIE	13
LEAH	That's unlucky
SOPHIE	12
LEAH	12?
SOPHIE	Give me a run up to 10. Give me a run up to 10.
LEAH	12
	11
	10

                    9

                    8

                    7

                    6

                    5

                    4

                    3

                    2

                    1

                    .

                    .

                    .

SOPHIE remains on the trampoline.

          Ok that's fine, that's fine. Not a problem. Let's try
          again.

                    10

SOPHIE   12

LEAH   10

SOPHIE   12

LEAH   10

                    9

                    8

                    7

                    6

5

4

3

2

1

GO

AND GO

.

.

.

SOPHIE remains on the trampoline.

LEAH   That's alright, third time lucky. Those were your warm ups. Just throw those away. Throw them away. This is the one.

This is the one.

This is the one. Come on. COME ON. Ok.

10

9

8

5

6

5

4

3

2

1

AND GO.

AND GO.

AND GO.

AND GO.

AND GO.

AND GO.

AND GO.

AND GO.

AND GO.

AND GO.

AND GO.

AND GO.

AND GO.

AND GO.

AND GO.

AND GO.

AND GO.

AND GO.

AND GO.

AND GO.

AND GO.

AND GO.

AND GO.

SOPHIE   It's not working.

LEAH   AND GO.

SOPHIE   It's not working.

LEAH   AND GO.

SOPHIE   It's not working.

LEAH   AND GO.

SOPHIE   It's not working.

          .

LEAH   I've got an idea. This is a knife. *(She is referring to the microphone.)*

          Imagine this is a knife.

SOPHIE   Right.

LEAH   On the floor you're safe. The floor is safe.
          Here *(pointing to trampoline)* you're not safe.
          (Ominously, into mic.) She's killed here before.

SOPHIE   Who?

          .

          .

          .

LEAH charges at SOPHIE holding microphone as if it's a knife, making wild stabbing gestures at SOPHIE.

SOPHIE remains on trampoline.

Improvised attacking from LEAH and reaction from SOPHIE.

37

LEAH   It's working!

SOPHIE   Who are you though?

LEAH   It doesn't matter who I am. All you need to know is that I'm on crack.

LEAH charges again. Improvised attacking from LEAH and reaction from SOPHIE.

SOPHIE remains on trampoline.

Ok, I'm going to surprise you. Don't look at me.

LEAH creeps behind her, then jumps out.

(Into mic.) You better run for your fucking life.

SOPHIE   I don't like it I don't like it.

It's not working.

.

LEAH   5, 4, 3, 2, 1

SOPHIE   Leah it's not working.

LEAH   54321!

SOPHIE   Leah.

LEAH   That's a shame. That's a shame Sophie. You were nearly there.

SOPHIE   I wasn't nearly there.

7B.

LEAH   *(Drawn back to the puzzle.)* There's a lot more side pieces in this one than I thought there was. *(Finding a piece.)* Tiny fox. Teeny fox! Where's he been hiding?

SOPHIE   Leah.

LEAH   But –

SOPHIE   .

LEAH   Ok, no. I've got it. I've got it.

She takes her chair over to the trampoline. Stands on chair.

We're gonna do something now that you're not going to like. Do you want to do it?

SOPHIE   What is it?

LEAH slaps SOPHIE.

Fucking hell!

LEAH   That was it.

We're going to make this space a negative space, a space you don't want to be anymore.

SOPHIE   No!

LEAH   Listen, listen, *(stumbling)* there's really successful – high success rates for this sort of thing, if you just – it's the kind of – I read about it in –

SOPHIE   Just do it. Just do it.

LEAH slaps SOPHIE continuously. These should be real. No stage combat.

Stop it.

LEAH   Is it working?

SOPHIE   Am I off it?

LEAH slaps SOPHIE continuously on the other cheek.

Stop it!

LEAH   Do you want to try again?

SOPHIE   Are you enjoying this?

LEAH   No!

LEAH slaps SOPHIE continuously on both cheeks.

SOPHIE   Stop it! I'm done. I'm done.

LEAH   Oh Sophie, don't be like that.

No answer.

You're going to get through this. You're going to get through this – ok wait.

7C.

LEAH signals to Rachel in the tech box, to play a particular song.

'Don't Give Up' by Peter Gabriel plays.

LEAH   Just listen

.

.

.

.

.

.

.

.

(To Rachel.) It's quite a long intro isn't it. Should we fast forward? No? No? Ok.

SOPHIE   What are you –

LEAH   Just wait.

                .

                .

                .

                .

                .

                .

                .

            They wait awkwardly through the intro, then the verse, until
            the chorus. LEAH lipsyncs the song to SOPHIE.

            Don't give up
            'Cause you have friends

SOPHIE   Fucking hell.

LEAH   Don't give up
            You're not beaten yet
            Don't give up
            I know you can make it good

SOPHIE   Stop it. Turn it off. Leah, turn it off right now.

            Rachel, turn it off, Rachel –

        Music stops.

            What are you doing?

LEAH   It's Peter Gabriel.

                .

SOPHIE   I know it's Peter Gabriel. Why are you playing
            me Peter Gabriel?

LEAH   Featuring Kate Bush.

41

Have you seen the video? *(Miming Peter Gabriel and Kate Bush holding each other as in the music video.)* They're just turning and holding –

SOPHIE   D'you think this is funny? Am I a joke to you?

LEAH   No

SOPHIE   D'you know what? It's fine. I'm fine.

.

.

.

.

8.

LEAH   You're not fine.

SOPHIE   I am.

LEAH   You're not.

SOPHIE   I'm fine.

LEAH   You're not fine.

SOPHIE   I'm fine.

LEAH   You're not fine.

SOPHIE   I am, I'm fine.

LEAH   You're not fine.

SOPHIE   I'm fine.

LEAH   You're not fine.

SOPHIE   I'm fine.

LEAH   You're not fine.

SOPHIE   I'm fine! I'm fine! I'm fine!

SOPHIE gets off the trampoline, walks around the space as if she's fine, then goes straight back on the trampoline.

LEAH   What?

What?

That wasn't fine! That wasn't fine.

.

You're not fine.

.

.

.

Ok. You're fine are you?

LEAH goes and gets a glass and fills if with water. She hands it to SOPHIE.

SOPHIE   Thank you.

SOPHIE bounces on the trampoline with the open glass of water. The water goes everywhere, on SOPHIE and on the floor. SOPHIE attempts to drink it. Hands what is left of the water back to LEAH.

LEAH   Don't you want to finish it?

SOPHIE   Yep.

She finishes the water. More spillage. Worse. She hands the glass back to LEAH.

That was very refreshing, thank you.

.

.

.

LEAH grabs a towel or blue roll from Rachel in tech box and mops up the water that went on the trampoline and floor.

LEAH   Is this fine? Is this fine Sophie?

SOPHIE   Yeah

LEAH   You're not fine, Sophie you're not fine.

SOPHIE   *(Snaps.)* I'M FINE. I'M FINE.

.

.

.

LEAH   You'll miss leaving

SOPHIE   No I won't

.

.

LEAH   You'll miss your train home.

SOPHIE   Happy here.

.

.

LEAH   You'll miss fresh air

SOPHIE   It's overrated.

.

.

LEAH   You'll miss seeing people here in the bar later.

SOPHIE   No I won't. *(To audience.)* No offence.

LEAH   You'll miss the sunset.

You'll miss watching people on the public transport.

You'll miss sitting in the sun with a newspaper you won't finish reading and a whole day stretching out ahead of you like an untouched sandy beach.

You'll miss stepping into a house and trying to work out if it's where you want to live.

You'll miss the entire world outside as it wonders where you are then forgets.

You'll miss packed lunches up mountains.

You'll miss running in the rain.

You'll miss road trips.

You'll miss grass.

You'll miss the foetal position.

You'll miss late night visits to the 24hr shop.

You'll miss late night visits to the snack cupboard.

You'll miss a billion tiny acts of vast generosity.

You'll miss the next war.

You'll miss the next terrorist attack.

You'll miss the next drone strike.

You'll miss the next grainy video of the next severed head.

You'll miss trying to make sense of why people do such awful, awful things to one another.

You'll miss the sky changing colour as the chemical make-up of the atmosphere changes.

You'll miss the landing on Mars.

You'll miss being there for your parents as they grow forgetful and ill.

You'll miss tapas.

.

.

.

SOPHIE   I'm fine.

LEAH   Fine.

LEAH walks away changes her mind and then pulls SOPHIE off the trampoline.

9.

Physical sequence of LEAH pulling and pushing SOPHIE off the trampoline. Improvised text. Increasing anger from SOPHIE throughout until –

SOPHIE   IF YOU DON'T BACK OFF, YOU ARE GOING TO REGRET IT.

LEAH   I'm going to regret it? What are you going to do? What are you going to do? Are you going to chase me around the room?

SOPHIE   Seriously.

LEAH   Ok. Fine.

SOPHIE continues to bounce on the trampoline. LEAH pretends to go back to the puzzle. LEAH creeps up behind SOPHIE. Whilst SOPHIE is mid-bounce in the air, LEAH pulls the trampoline from underneath her. SOPHIE lands on the ground.

Stillness.

SOPHIE looks at the floor.

SOPHIE looks at LEAH.

SOPHIE looks at LEAH's Masterpiece Puzzle. LEAH looks at her Masterpiece puzzle, back to SOPHIE.

SOPHIE begins to walk towards it. LEAH stops her mid-walk.

Sophie.

SOPHIE tries to get to the puzzle. LEAH tries to restrain her. They wrestle. A proper fight. Text where necessary, 'Please don't' etc.

SOPHIE gets away and destroys LEAH's puzzle.

Furious, SOPHIE gets back on the trampoline.

10.

LEAH, broken, withdraws to the back of the room.

SOPHIE bounces.

LEAH forces herself to look at the destroyed puzzle pieces on the floor.

She begins the process of picking them up.

SOPHIE watches.

Whilst maintaining the bounce on the trampoline, SOPHIE retrieves the mic cable off the floor. Using the cable, she pulls the mic stand slowly towards her, unseen by LEAH.

SOPHIE attempts to sing something into the microphone whilst bouncing. This is difficult. She adjusts the mic to a level where she can sing parts of the song as she reaches the maximum height of her jump.

A game for the performer to negotiate.

SOPHIE   This land is your land, this land is my land
          From California, to the New York Island
          From the Redwood Forest, to the Gulf Stream
          waters
          This land was made for you and me.

          This land was made for you and me.

LEAH watches. She takes the mic away.

11.

SOPHIE watches LEAH sorting pieces.

SOPHIE gets off the trampoline.

She picks up a missed puzzle piece off the floor and offers it to LEAH.

LEAH looks at her, then withdraws again to the back of the room.

SOPHIE looks at the puzzle, looks at the trampoline.

She moves over to the puzzle station and turns on the lamp. It's not working. She twists the bulb. It comes on.

She looks at the puzzle, and attempts to start.

SOPHIE   If I find bits of sky, what do I...

          And animals, if I put them...

          If I come across a human, what do I do? Do I put
          them in man/woman piles or do I put them together?

LEAH   Together.

          .

          .

          .

SOPHIE   *(Holding a piece up to the light.)* What's that?

    LEAH reluctantly moves towards SOPHIE to look at the piece.

LEAH   **Hay bale on fire**

    .

    .

    .

SOPHIE   *(Holding another piece up to the light.)* What's that?

LEAH   **Brussel sprout**.

    .

    .

    .

    We need to start by separating all the side pieces.

    Together, they separate side pieces.

12.

They find two connecting pieces.

SOPHIE   Oh.

    It's a connection.

    SOPHIE looks at Rachel in the tech box.

    LEAH notices.

LEAH   No

    It's too late.

    'Ain't that Terrible' by Rod Redmond plays.

SOPHIE begins a tiny version of their usual celebration dance.

Initially SOPHIE does this on her own, until LEAH is slowly persuaded to join in, until they do a tiny version of the dance, together.

13A.

Music stops. LEAH continues with the puzzle, in some way restored.

SOPHIE looks at the trampoline. She continues separating side pieces.

LEAH   Ooo, no, this is good, there's the runaway steam train in the background of the picture that's ploughing through the fairground, there's quite a few dead bodies around. We can start with those because they're quite easy to find.

.

.

.

.

.

Ah. What d'you think that is?

SOPHIE   A goat.

LEAH   Oh yeah, I can see why you might think that.

But if you look at it this way. It could also be a cat.

Couldn't it?

It could also be a cat couldn't it?

SOPHIE	Yeah.
LEAH	What d'you think? Cat or goat?
SOPHIE	I don't know.
LEAH	Yeah but if you had to choose
SOPHIE	I don't know, it could be either
LEAH	Yeah but if you had to choose
SOPHIE	I said I don't –
LEAH	You've got a gun to your head. Cat or goat?
SOPHIE	Goat.

.

.

Probably a goat.

.

.

LEAH	Correct.

13B.

LEAH	What are you working on? No, they don't fit together. No, no, don't, huuuuh. *(SOPHIE jams them together.)* No, no, no, no, no. Sophie don't jam them, don't jam them together. Be careful. You've got to be careful. It's a careful man's game.

13C.

LEAH	What about this one?

.

.

Sophie, what about this one?

.

.

What about that one?

SOPHIE   What about that one?

LEAH   If you had to allocate that within the system,
          where would it go? Where would it go?

SOPHIE   Object.

LEAH   Hmm. That's interesting, why d'you say that?

SOPHIE   Because it's a balloon.

LEAH   Right.

.

It is a balloon.

But it's also got a face on it. So in a way, is it
human?

SOPHIE   But it's still on a balloon.

LEAH   Yeah, you're right.

          But then again, what if it is a man but he has a
          balloon for a face. Look at the expression, that's a
          real expression, the mischievous grin.

SOPHIE   Human then.

LEAH   But it is still a balloon.

SOPHIE   Balloon then.

LEAH   Or a balloon man.

SOPHIE   Human then.

LEAH   But is a balloon man a man, or a balloon??

          .

          .

          .

          .

SOPHIE   Does it matter?

LEAH   Yes, it matters hugely.

SOPHIE   What did you do last time?

LEAH   We're a team now.

SOPHIE   Yes.

LEAH   So what do you think? Object or human?

SOPHIE   Object.

LEAH   Really?

          Really?

          Really?

SOPHIE   What do you think it is? Object or Human.

LEAH   Human. Come on Sophie, it's obvious.

          .

          .

          .

          .

          .

(Finding a new piece.) Oooooh! FOUND IT!
Found you! You little shit. You little shit. God,
this piece evaded me for so long last time. But
now I know, I know, it's a beak. It's a beak. Big
in the foreground. The rest of the bird is behind
the grass, so I couldn't – This is good, this is
good. We're refining the process, re-hauling the
process, turning over the soil. Now I know some
of the answers but are their more questions to
ask? Are there more questions to ask?

This piece, I thought that was wallpaper for so
long last time, now I KNOW it's corrugated iron. I
know it's corrugated iron, part of the roof, bottom
left. This is so exciting! Sophie, I've never done
this before, we're going to redevelop it, Sophie?

*SOPHIE is back on the trampoline. She stands on it. Begins
a slow bounce, until it becomes bigger, until it returns to
her usual full bounce.*

Long silence.

.

.

.

.

.

.

.

.

.

.

·

·

·

·

·

·

·

Sophie. That's it now.

LEAH resets the space, so she is able to begin her puzzle process again.

·

·

14.

LEAH   Date. *(Say whatever date it is.)* Commencing re-completion of 939B.

Piece 1.

Mainly features **an angry dog, behind bars**…

She stops – listening to bouncing.

Piece 2.

Ah I remember this piece from last time. It's part of the bull's head from the –

She stops – listening to bouncing.

·

·

·

·

·

·

·

·

·

·

·

·

·

LEAH takes her jumper off and wraps it around her head to block out the sound of the trampoline.

She tries to ignore the sound for a long as possible until –

She looks at SOPHIE.

SOPHIE   I'm sorry.

LEAH   Yeah?

         Are you sorry?

         Are you?

         Because this is not fair. It's not fair.

SOPHIE   You don't understand.

         ·

LEAH   You don't understand.

SOPHIE   You don't understand.

LEAH   You don't understand.

SOPHIE   You – you don't understand Leah.

LEAH   No you don't understand. You don't understand.

SOPHIE   You don't understand.

LEAH   You don't understand.

SOPHIE   You don't understand.

Repeat this, improvised, until –

15.

LEAH   You don't understand that I don't care.

I actually don't care that you're stuck on that thing.

If I've shown you that I care, I've done that, I've done that, because it's easier. I've done that because, in some way, it's better for me, easier for me. I've done that, because that's what people do. That's what people – I've done that because I have to. Those are the rules, those are the rules of civilised – Because if I didn't, if I didn't – you'd find me out. *(To the audience.)* They'd all find me out. I'd be caught red-handed.

A man asks me for change on the street. Don't care. Friend's been cheated on. Don't care. I've betrayed you. Don't care. I can't contemplate your feelings. I can't contemplate you. You don't exist. You don't exist in that moment. You don't exist. *(To the audience.)* None of you exist. It's just me. It's just me here. It's just – Thousands are killed everyday. Don't care. Not real. Bombings. Don't care. Abductions. Don't care.

To audience.

I don't care about the boy on the beach.

I don't care about the refugees on the boats.

I don't care about detention centres.

I don't care that you fell over at your job interview.

I don't care that you're going bald.

I don't care that you feel undesired.

I don't care that you've got low self-esteem.

I don't care that you sometimes think about walking out in front of a car just to feel something.

I don't care about

I fucking do not care about if you've done a marathon.

I do not care if you've been in the London marathon.

I don't care if you've done a 10k.

I don't care what your time was.

Literally, do not tell me about it.

Don't tell me that you're working on some project.

That you're feeling motivated.

That you've changed your lifestyle.

That you've become a fucking yoga instructor.

That you're qualifying as a yoga instructor now.

No I'm not going to come to one of your taster sessions.

Absolutely not.

I'm not coming.

I don't care that you think you're fat.

I don't care that your grandma died.

I don't care that your dog died.

I don't care about climate change.

I don't care about nuclear weapons.

I don't care about poverty.

I don't care about recycling.

I don't care about hacking.

I don't care about fracking.

I don't know what it is.

I don't know what it is.

I don't care about fossil fuels running out.

I don't care about suicide, I don't care about genocide, I don't care about mass murder.

I couldn't care less about Kristallnacht.

I don't care about gender equality.

I don't care that you think change is happening too slowly.

I don't care about the woman who is in court at the moment.* I don't care about her. Don't give a shit.

I don't care about the fact you always do the washing-up.

I don't care that it's always you buying the washing-up liquid.

I don't care that you're lonely.

I don't care about unethical farming.

I don't care about your vegan diet.

I don't care about your bad back
                        fox hunting
                        gentrification
                        privatisation
                        your children
                        your holiday
                        your divorce
                        that your eczemas come
                        back
                        that you've only got £100
                        in your bank to see you
                        through the whole month.

I don't care about your overdraft
                        your debt
                        your god
                        your nutribullet
                        quinoa
                        junior doctors
                        single use plastic
                        microbeads
                        terrorism
                        the second referendum*
                        that you had a hard day
                        that Bowie* died.

I don't care about what you think they think about you, that no
one laughs at your jokes. I don't care that you lost your wallet,
                        lost your phone
                        lost your dignity.

I don't care that you've lost hope
                        that you've lost faith
                        that you've lost face
                        that you've lost your favourite jacket.

I don't care you feel like a lemon
                    a gooseberry
                    a third wheel
                    a slug
                    a wet blanket
                    a keen bean
                    a tired old misery guts.

I don't care about your veruca
I don't care about your wart
                    your cist
                    your zit
                    your swelling
                    your bruise
                    your scratch
                    your cancer
                    your ulcer
the scab that you keep picking until it bleeds.

your varicose veins
your bitten   nails
your split   ends
your paper   cut
your sun   burn
I don't care that you're infertile.

I don't care that you're bleeding.

I don't care that you're sweating profusely even
though you've only walked up one flight of the
stairs.

I don't care that you're going blind.

I don't care that you don't sleep at night. I've got
nothing to say to that.

I don't care about your dreams.

Do not tell me about the dream you had last night. I'm not interested.

I don't care about your dreams dying.

I don't care about the person stamping on all your dreams.

I don't care if you think that person is me.

I care about this. *(Referencing puzzle.)*
This is what I care about.
This is all I care about.

SOPHIE   I do exist.

LEAH   No you don't.

SOPHIE   I do.

LEAH   You don't.

SOPHIE   I do –

LEAH   I actually don't care that you're stuck on that thing. What I care about is that sound. That sound in my head. Stopping me from doing what I need to do.

16.

LEAH moves the trampoline, with SOPHIE on it, into the corner.

SOPHIE   What are you doing? Leah what are you doing?

LEAH   *(To Rachel in the tech box.)* Can we turn the lights off on her?

SOPHIE   Please, no please don't. I'll stop.

LEAH   Yeah? Ok. Cool.

.

.

.

.

Go on.

SOPHIE   Just give me a minute!

LEAH   Ok, you have one minute.

(To Rachel.) And then can we take that away and dismantle it?

Yeah, you have one minute and then we're going to take it away.

(Using the stopwatch on her phone to time.) Starting…now.

The one minute countdown begins.

Halfway through, SOPHIE gets off and stands on the floor, tense.

LEAH goes to take the trampoline away. SOPHIE stops her. They wait.

SOPHIE   How long have I got left?

LEAH   17 seconds.

.

.

10

.

.

3, 2, 1.

The minute is up. SOPHIE remains on the floor. LEAH goes to take the trampoline away. SOPHIE stops her. There is a standoff. LEAH tries to get past her once more.

SOPHIE goes back on to the trampoline. She carries on bouncing.

LEAH looks to Rachel.

Rachel.

Lights go out. The lamp remains on, lighting the puzzle, but SOPHIE is in the dark. SOPHIE bounces in the darkness.

SOPHIE   No, no, no.

Please, Leah. Give me one more minute. Let me try again.

LEAH sets herself back up at the puzzle station.

LEAH!

LEAH   *(To Rachel.)* Can we get some music please?

Music plays. 'Modern Love' by David Bowie. Loud – it drowns out the sound of SOPHIE's pleas.

LEAH continues with the puzzle. She talks about the pieces to the audience through the mic. We see her lips moving but we probably cannot hear her over the music.

.

.

.

.

.

.

After some time, she stops.

She looks back into the darkness at SOPHIE.

She looks at the lamp.

She points the lamp back at SOPHIE.

SOPHIE bounces on the trampoline, lit by the desk lamp.

LEAH and SOPHIE look at each other.

End.